At a Loss

POEMS

At a Loss

POEMS

2008–2023

CALLIE REVELL

For Sam

*My light—not at the end of the tunnel,
but in the middle, where it's darkest.*

Contents

Acknowledgments

With heartfelt humility, I express my sincerest gratitude.

First, of course, to Sam, my husband of twelve years and friend for much longer. My Believer, who never questions my talent but only questions its whereabouts when it hides away and hibernates. My confidence soars through your eyes. These words are my gift to you and a receipt for what I took (so much inspiration). Thank you for encouraging me during my insecure moments when I considered keeping this all to myself. You make me courageous. I love you so much.

To my boys, Greyson and Stellan, who are too

young to read this and will be for a long time. If you ever do decide to dive into your mother's thoughts, I hope you'll know they are a product of many emotional moments that often diminished with time. Any hardship I've experienced being your mom has been eclipsed a thousand times over by the joy, pride, and fulfillment you've brought me. I love you both so much that my definition of love has changed since you came into my life.

To Dr. Bob Fink, the one who taught me how to harness the magic of words: your voice echoed in my head often while writing, and I imagined myself more than once in the workshop circle on a Tuesday night, reading aloud to a group of fellow poets. Your impact on my life, though largely unspoken, has not been overlooked.

To Ian, Jeremy, Camille, and Meghan: thank you for taking time out of your lives to read these first and make sure I wasn't just littering. Your feedback was invaluable and gave me courage. Much love to you.

Thank you specifically to Camille for your brilliance and beautiful reflections and especially for your help with the phonetic alphabet, which has always been a puzzle to me.

And a note in particular to Jeremy: for all those nights spent at Java City or out on the school lawn when you listened to my poetry before it was even good (before it was even anything), thank you. You were the first in my life to really listen. I love you.

To my wonderful parents and beautiful sisters, the ones I have *not* lost through good times and bad, thank you for sticking with me and sticking together. Our storms have not yet passed, but our fortress is strong, and we will come out the other side. Thank you for reading the poems I wrote as a seven-year-old about snowmen and bunny rabbits and the colors of the rainbow; thank you for tolerating my moody teenage poet phase when I thought I knew everything; and thank you for reading these poems now, in which I explain in many different ways that I know nothing.

To those featured in these stories—named or unnamed—thank you for allowing me to craft my experience with you into something that can heal me. Chances are, though, I didn't ask for your permission, so I'd like to go ahead and apologize for that.

These poems were written between 2008 and 2023. Fifteen years is a long time to accumulate poems. They are not presented in chronological order. I may not feel the same emotions now that I did fifteen years ago (and I'm glad I don't). Many years of growth take place within these pages.

ACKNOWLEDGMENTS

Some of these poems were previously published or featured in: my senior capstone chapbook for Hardin-Simmons University, *The Healing Under Highway 20*; Hardin-Simmons University's literary arts magazine, *The Corral*; *Blackwing*, a passion collection for Dr. Fink by his former students; and my short-lived and well-meaning but ultimately insignificant blog, *The Dead Letter Diaries*.

Lastly, if you bought this book or have read even a single page of it, thank you with my whole heart. That's what we all hope for, isn't it? Someone to listen to what we have to say and not pretend to pay attention.

Introduction

In 2012, after graduating from college, I hit a severe case of writer's block. For the first time in my life, I wasn't in a structured school setting on a consistent basis. Without an academic schedule and the comforting presence of friends, I drifted away from my once-religious journaling habit, and I stopped finding poetry hiding around every corner. I poured myself into my media business and then into my children when my first arrived in 2017.

For seven years, I found myself at a literal loss for words.

During that time, life kept happening, of

course, and often in a blurry, fast-forward way. I missed a lot as I struggled through depression, anxiety, and then the struggles of becoming a parent. I spent most of my twenties like this—in a sort of fog with bursts of bright light.

The most personal loss came in November of 2019 when I was twenty-nine years old and had a miscarriage. That word still brings a jolt to my stomach. Anyone I talked to about it used terms like "lost the baby" or "experienced a pregnancy loss." Like I'd rolled the dice and came up short. Or like I had lost something I could never find again. It's still so painful to talk about or even think about, and it's a subject most people avoid, even though it's more common than I ever realized. I know that every emotion related to a miscarriage is valid: some people feel relieved, some feel disappointed, some feel nothing. I felt crushing, suffocating grief. I desperately clung to that baby until the very end when the doctor told me I was no longer pregnant (with four haunting words: "your uterus is empty"). But although I held on as tight as I could, some things are out of our control. After that happened, I boarded up my mind for the better part of a year.

Finally, words began to trickle out again, until the loss of my grandfather in August of 2023 burst the dam open. I wrote my poem, "Grief Is a Loyal

Dog," in September of 2023, and within the coming weeks, I would write thirty-four of the poems featured in this book. So, half of the poems in this collection took me fifteen years to write, and the other half took three weeks. The poems I wrote in those three weeks are ones that had been dormant in my heart for all those years, so they truly filled in that missing gap in my life.

You'll see several different styles of poetry in this book, and they represent the different phases I have gone through as a poet. Some of the poems are structured, rhyming villanelles, while others are abstract stream of consciousness. I still write in all styles, but my current preference is narrative free verse, which you'll see featured heavily here. As I've mentioned, the poems in this collection are not presented in chronological order, so you might read one from 2008 next to one from 2023. They are all me, just different versions of me.

I'm not the type of poet to preach at you; I'll let you draw your own conclusions and pull your own morals. I just want to tell you stories, either from my imagination or from my memories. I want you to feel how I felt.

Memories are precious to me, especially after witnessing my mother-in-law, Sue, lose all of her memories to Alzheimer's disease before passing away in 2014. She took so many memories with her that I never got to hear. Much of this book consists of my memories and the memories of those I love.

At a Loss encompasses my desperate grasping for words when I couldn't find them, but it also details my journey finding myself at a loss again and again. I have stumbled upon loss after loss of people or things or places that have been so precious to me.

I don't believe I've experienced more significant amounts of grief than the average person—I'm fortunate and understand that many have had it much worse than me. But grief is a universal concept across every culture, and every single person has lost someone or something.

I want to remember the ones I've lost: three of my four grandparents, my mother-in-law, a mentor, a pet, a friend, my baby. This doesn't even include the friends I've lost to time, distance, or conflict—friends I still think about often and miss terribly. But death in particular has taken some very precious people from me.

And more will come. That's how it goes. You lose and lose until everyone else loses you.

But when you choose, like I did, to keep it all in—to refuse to talk about it or write about it or even think about it—it starts to consume you. It takes too much of your heart and puts it on the other side where they are. It keeps you torn in two.

So, I have to turn the pain into art somehow. It's how I manage. I'm not sure how everyone else does, but we all do, in our own way.

W.H. Auden once wrote, "You owe it to all of us to get on with what you're good at." That's what I'm attempting to do here, finally, for the first time in a long time.

To those who have lost Someone or Something that left a crater behind, I hope you find some sort of comfort in these pages and in the knowledge that I, a kindred spirit, am one of many. Your pain is not a weakness. It can bloom in its own season.

Callie Revell
November 10, 2023

One writes of scars healed, a loose parallel to the pathology of the skin, but there is no such thing in the life of an individual. There are open wounds, shrunk sometimes to the size of a pin-prick but wounds still. The marks of suffering are more comparable to the loss of a finger, or of the sight of an eye. We may not miss them, either, for one minute in a year, but if we should there is nothing to be done about it.

F. Scott Fitzgerald

TENDER IS THE NIGHT

I.

I Can't Take That Name Again

Hello

We step from a shower onto tile,
letting a puddle gather at our feet
and follow us to a damp rug.
We place both hands on a marble countertop
and breathe steam into our lungs.
Our shoulders sag.

We preoccupy ourselves
with toothpaste, lotion, running water
from a tap that drips at night,
a cream to keep us young,
a brush clumped with dull, dead hair.

The mirror is a blur.

We wait for the water droplets
to cling, trail down the glass
in perfect parallel lines.

Or, out of impatience,
we sweep a handprint—

Our eyes lock.
Once friends,
now meeting by chance
on an unfamiliar street,

averting eyes,

realizing how awkward
it would be to say hello.

Lakebed

I used to think in lilted language
like snowflakes drifting lazily down,
getting caught in tree branches
and gathering in windswept drifts.

Now my thoughts drop like hailstones
on the glassy surface of a dark lake,
falling too quickly to count,
too slick to catch,
stinging when they strike.

Who will gather hailstones
from the lakebed
and place them in my arms
for me to rock to sleep?

When You First Walk In

When you first walk in
after a long trip
and your house has that
borrowed smell,
that tentative unfamiliarity,

it only means that you
are not the same as you were
when you left.

Drop your keys on the table.
Hang your coat on the hook.
Your name is on all the envelopes, and
no one has stopped by to dust.

Nevermind
your heavier posture,
your dragging feet—
this is still your Place.

The discomfort fades away
after an hour or so
as the smell retreats
back into the walls,
waiting for you
to leave again.

Kites and Clocks

I can't believe it's been a year—
silver stillness hangs in the air.
The seams that separate us tear,
the world suspended in a tear.

The phrase to which we're now attuned:
"I once was lost, but now I'm found."
The date is set, the clock is wound,
we press our palms against the wound.

"I see your point," he calmly said,
but there's greed in every good deed—
the saddest thing you'll ever read,
the greatest truth I've ever read.

The truth about the lies of love:
the bold intricacies we wove,
and how we ducked and dimly dove
on the wilted wings of a dove.

Although I smirk, I don't suppose
I could handle a heavy dose.
You know, I've never been this close
to watching pages start to close.

I hate to say this, but you'll find
some missing pieces in the end:
you'll watch the kites without the wind,
and there will still be clocks to wind.

It's hard to say just what I need.
It's fabricated in my head:
a bullet is just lifeless lead,
and yet, it always takes the lead.

Silver Streak

For years, it was my
fun fact I would share
during uncomfortable
icebreaker games:

I have a silver streak of hair
sprouting from my left temple.
It magically appeared one morning
when I was fourteen.

My friends would joke about
my superpowers,
and I would twist it and
pin it back to show it off.

But one night, I found an article
about the effects of stress in
young teenagers, and I saw
a boy with a patch of silver
in his short-cropped hair.

And I thought of you, then,
behind me in study hall
in eighth grade,
passing me those notes,
tracing my shoulders with
your pencil eraser,
whispering questions you
knew I couldn't answer.

And I doubt you remember, but
freshman year, I left the bus

in tears that day.

The scar you left will fade
when I get old enough.

I looked up your picture.
Your hair is still brown.

Musca Domestica

We murmur prayers against your pestilence
and never-ending swarms, punishing your
posterity, cursing your creation.
You huddle over rancid carcasses and,
in the heat, you stick to mud and slime,
calling your friends, feasting in the sunshine
while someone somewhere mourns.

Born as a wriggling, repulsive maggot
into a webbed world, a flimsy fragile
body left alone to battle giants.
Your heart is a pinprick, your blood a drop.
A life as short as yours is spent unwisely
huddled on heaps of festering garbage.

Someone once told me I would never hurt you,
but I've heartlessly killed your kind before
and it didn't feel quite like murder should.

Here, in this room, I hear you buzzing in
blind hysteria behind dusty drapes,
seeking escape, tapping on taunting glass.
The pages of my book fall closed and I
just blink, understanding how you're feeling,
envying your tiny, papery wings.

Goodnight, Analog

If they pull the switch on us tonight,
if the blackouts leave us barely blind,
I'll face the darkness with an open mind.
I've never seen the stars so bright.

We've been sitting on this couch too long;
my eyes burn from artificial light.
If the television tells it right,
then you and I both have it wrong.

If the lights go out while we eat,
plastic silverware won't stay strong.
I'll calmly say, "I knew it all along."
Neighbors gather wide-eyed in the street.

In the sudden silence, I will stand.
You'll still be frozen in your seat,
waiting for the darkness to retreat.
At the end of the world, I'll hold your hand.

You know, there's freedom in the flight;
technology was never completely kind.
The Sentence of Sinners has been signed,
but I can't seem to feel contrite.

My Mind Collapsed Into Dust Like a Star

at a loss for words
I turn instead
to self-destruction

in the panic I feel
       the weight of my own
       inadequacy
I feign indifference

a quiet voice tells me
I'm faking it for attention
       pathetic pitiful wretch

and I can only hope
my planets will survive
the implosion

       dark dark dark
       all descends into dark
       screens and matches
       fluorescent light bulbs
       paper lanterns
       cigarettes

at a loss for words
I turn instead
to silence

The Bottom of My Jones Soda Bottle Cap

said,
"Write a poem."

The carbonated sugar
crackled on my tongue.

"Write a poem!"
I scoffed to my
empty passenger seat,
as if a genie had erupted
from the bottle
demanding three wishes
of his own.

I screwed the cap back on,
tossed the glass in the back seat,

the last swig of root beer
fermenting in the filtered sun,

surfacing a tiny,
swaying ship.

To Noah Veil, A Man With a Mouth

He uttered words with shrugs and sighs,
and arguments fell on deaf ears.
Around his face, the room would fade,
with evidence flooding his eyes.
> When a man speaks, he seldom hears;
> any progress we might've made
> was easily resigned to fail,
> and so I spoke to Noah Veil.

He'd climb up on his chair to say,
"Yes, time is like a turning wheel."
His voice would keep me wide awake:
what drives a man to speak that way?
> I tore the curtains to reveal
> my most obvious mistake.
> My skin felt thin, my face grew pale;
> I gave my trust to Noah Veil.

I've wasted so much time with tears,
pacing on the steps for too long.
It's getting harder to pretend
that I am strong and have no fears,
that I am seldom ever wrong.
> It's always tough to trust an end.
> The tears on my cheeks left a trail,
> and so I wept to Noah Veil.

A sucker for a sacrifice
will always have a life to save,
and flowers sliced at the stem
will always fetch the highest price.

We have microphones, yet we crave
the sound of one old-fashioned hymn,
and from the back pew, I would wail,
"I gave my life to Noah Veil."

Perhaps it's part of the journey.
The next adventure is the sun,
but the clock will chime at midnight.
You'll be rushed off on a gurney,
and reality will come undone.
Remember, love is worth the fight;
so, I will fight this tooth and nail,
and still I write to Noah Veil.

Elucidation

I. medicinema
/ˈme-də-ˈsən-nə-mə/

a velvet rope fences in the crowd
he grips a ticket as his
mother skims the running time and
promises to wait in the car

"Take your Adderal so you won't fidget."
a large popcorn balanced
on his lap and he gives cheap laughs

the pills are powerless to those
who were faking it all along
who made us seem just as strong
to come out on top in the end

it's all for the sake of the show

just dim the lights and set the scene
let the speakers swell the soundtrack
splash color on a silver screen

II. whimpact
/ˈwim-pakt/

ideas spontaneously spark
and suddenly make perfect sense

go ahead and say how you feel
but don't expect them to take notes

argue them into excellence
if they ask pointed questions

your brilliance will be waved away
in the name of social science

with blank stares shooting into space
it all goes downhill after this

III. dollarson
/ˈdäl-ˈär-sən/

my avarice avenges me
I want it every part of it

on the twenty-second story
they light their cigars with Hamiltons
they swap stories of the old days
and toast each other left-handed
nonchalantly judging watches
and making mental Christmas lists

IV. oxygenetics
/ˈäks-ə-jəˈn-e-tiks/

it's generated in my genes
it's starched and stitched into my seams

black ink blots in my history
just censor out the gruesome parts
and leave us gaping in the dark
but no one speaks of such things

our photos are all fading fast
each of us over-edited

lightning strikes my family tree
it sparks and smokes and burns and burns

V. dreaddition
/dre-ˈdi-shən/

the name tastes foreign to my tongue

I lived without you in my life
for twenty years but now you're here

I want to take my handshake back
and lose five minutes of my life
a slightly noble sacrifice
to brighten up a bitter end

I can't forget your name your face
is burned and branded on my brain
it stalks me slowly into sleep

VI. traumark
/ˈtrou-märk/

it's imprinted into my eyes
for you to read and analyze
the scar for showing off my heart
for never knowing when to run
just a target to practice on

I hate that it's so obvious

I can't destroy my own design
what happened here is permanent
I slip my feet out of my shoes
and dare to touch this sacred ground

I can't go back to who I was
and I can't take that name again

VII. fraudience
/ˈfrôd-ń-əns/

a thousand faces without eyes
read the expression on my face
the spotlight wipes my vision white

it seems too late to make a scene
but I don't have a script for this
my ticket reads 14C
an actress smirks up from my seat
I read her lips she feeds me lines

I hate the air that leaves my lungs
and rocks the rafters with my lies

which side which side to exit on

Assurance

I see her face and hear her voice
on an old VHS tape

I know her
we used to be friends
before all of this happened

in my mind
I find her playing
in the backyard pretending
ants are an invading army and
the acorns must protect their children

I drop to my knees
tuck her hair behind her ear
open my arms and
gather her into them

this girl who did nothing wrong
and didn't deserve it
who has no idea
how strong she'll be
when the time comes

Calamity

the words tap on my lips
    they fret in my brain
        I do not cannot know how to
            let them set them free

        I feel the air hot in my head
      it cracks open my brain cells
    the room at once too small
the air too thick caught in my throat

have you ever considered how
    the breath entering your lungs might've
        passed through the bronchial tubes
            of a dozen others in the crowd
        before they wrung out the oxygen
    and expelled the stale carbon dioxide
for you to gasp into yourself

the calamity plays out like a script
    me with my one line lost
        as they raise the lights
            look at the others they have talent

        now breathe a little slower just
      take it all in exhale inhale exhale
    hyper hyper don't panic ventilate

always take a second look here it
    whispers softly but I read lips
        I read books I read looks and
            I've seen that one so many times before

you go you stay you work for pay
your last check buried in the bank
it's mostly just to pass the time
you need more friends more lovers

the words know where they go
when my mind shuts down and my
eyes turn away when the day fades
my heart and I are faint acquaintances

and in the crowd I am
more alone than ever

Just Cut My Hair, Please

don't ask me how my day has been
or if it's still raining outside (it is)

don't ask me if I washed my hair
before I came (I didn't)

don't point out all the new hairs
sprouting by my neck and ears
(it's still not enough)

I just want to sit in silence
while you remove pieces of
myself I no longer need

As I Thumb Through *Norton's Anthology of American Literature, Shorter Sixth Edition*

I can't read,

not the way they need me to.
I constantly skim and skip
and drip like an overfull sponge.

The font: Fairfield Medium,
too small for my aching eyes.
I know they want me to
breathe deeply and
absorb their words through
fluttering eyelashes,
but I

get anxious in the middle,
bypass their art, flip the
2,853 delicate pages
just to see if they

have found a way
to solve the discord
and can teach me, too.

Curtains

Don't let the curtains sew themselves shut.

The shadows will sing you to sleep
and keep you dreamless to
tempt you into indifference.

Your dilated eyes will adjust too much,
and you'll forget what time it is, until
you don't care what time it is.

When you finally peek out through a gap,
the sun will feel too close to earth,
and you will retreat back into the darkness,

wondering,

is it selfish to hope the sun
will burn itself out
like they promised it would?

II.

There and Not Here

Seven Years

For Dr. Bob Fink, partly found from notes I can't throw away

A pencil poised above cheap 20-pound copy paper,
waiting to make contact, graphite flaking,
another stack waiting.

You have been a writer for a long time, haven't you?

A secret I omitted from our upbeat visits
and optimistic emails:
I've shelved the talent you said
would be a shame to waste,
shoved it into a top corner to
collect seven years of dust.

Try a more unique way of saying this.

I spent an entire year writing for three cents a word
about in-ground pools and Boy Scouts
and Habitat for Humanity,
sleeping 14 hours a day and eating too much cereal,
and then she finally died and I still had
nothing to say.

Make this more emphatic.

Now I charge by the word editing
books and blogs and résumés and dissertations—
scratching out the useless phrases,
but at least they've written something.

You use a lot of contractions.

And just last year I found myself
scrubbing milky vomit from the carpet at 3:00 a.m.,
a baby in my arms, both of us sobbing.
In the darkness, I whispered,
"I should've gone to grad school."

Maybe you don't need this either.

But that's the thing about books—
the dust adds character.
An ember still glows close to the spine,
and with one warm breath
I can burn the whole thing to ashes
and start again.

Are you sure you want to end it like this?

Qantas Flight 7 to DFW

HOUR ONE

We booked too late and ended up in
two middle seats in the middle row
of a Qantas Airbus A380.

1:10 p.m. in Sydney, and we're on time
to chase the sun into the
northern hemisphere.

HOUR SIX

I've watched the entire
Lord of the Rings trilogy
on the tiny screen in the
headrest of the seat in front of me.

We've eaten most of our snacks.

The man beside me smells like
salt and vinegar potato chips
and nicotine gum.

HOUR EIGHT

It should be dark by now,
and why *for the love of God*
does that woman in the window seat
have to read her book
in the blaring sunlight?

HOUR TEN

Neither of us has slept,
and it's still so bright.

Maybe the pilot is taking us
in circles over the Pacific.

HOUR THIRTEEN

I imagine we are humanity's last hope
crammed in this state-of-the-art spacecraft,
sent to colonize a distant, glowing planet.

They explained, by some scientific anomaly,
our 16 hours would actually be 34 years,
and though our bodies wouldn't age,
our minds would feel every second, so

to stave off the madness, they trained us to
watch the clouds out the simulated window
and think of home.

HOUR FIFTEEN

Somewhere over Mexico,
Sam gets a nosebleed
from the dry airplane air,

and the flight attendant
looks like she might cry
when she brings him
a stack of napkins.

HOUR SIXTEEN

1:45 p.m. in Dallas.

We only lost 35 minutes in the air,
and in the delirium, I wonder
if humans were ever meant to fly at all.

Troy Calling for Lacy

While we were playing after school,
my mother walked in
with the cordless phone
and gave it to me.

The voice in my ear
belonged to a boy,

a boy I had barely spoken to
and must've found my number
in the school directory
but wanted to talk to *me*.

I choked out a "hi,"
heart in my throat,
and he got straight
to the point:

"Is Lacy there?"

He knew my mother would've
told him not to call girls at
houses that aren't theirs.

Ten years later, I went on
my first ever date with a boy at
nineteen years old,
and that boy became my husband
pretty quickly after that.

I sometimes think about that little girl
handing the phone to her prettier friend,
telling her, "It's not for me.
It's for you."

Rolling Blackouts

During Winter Storm Uri, February 2021

They said the blackouts are for
the greater good,
that without them the entire grid
would be down for weeks,

so when we lose power the first time,
we pause and wait for it
to kick back on.

But after the third blackout,
the power doesn't come back
for three days.

Historically low temperatures
continue to drop:
23°F, 8°F,
-2°F—

The dog's water bowl freezes solid.
All of the faucets sputter and stop.
Even the snow outside
glosses over with ice,
echoing the cracking of
too-burdened tree branches.

At four in the morning,
we rouse the boys from sleep,
and we all take shelter
under the covers of our bed.

They drift off into a shivering slumber,

but I don't sleep—can't sleep—
watching the dog restless in the moonlight,
my son curled in his father's arms, shaking,
my two-month-old baby's breaths
coming in tiny puffs of fog.

Will we be like those families
found in Pompeii?
They knew what was coming
could not be outrun
and chose instead
to wait together.

Jake

While on a walk
in the glorious
Texas sunshine,
he pauses to smell
the summer grass,
laps up rainwater
from the gutter.

He sprawls across
the warm cement,
pink tongue dripping.

Despite the persistent
tug of a leash,
he stays.

Dark, shining eyes say,
"Carry me."

On Jeremy and Rebecca's Elopement

A judge married them
on a Wednesday morning
in a courtroom.

I drank their punch,
gave my hugs,
reveled in their contagious joy.

I helped carry boxes
into their new apartment.

If it were ours,
I would hang pictures of us
up the creaking staircase.
The floral print couch
we found at a yard sale
would go by the window.
I would stack our
chipped dishes in the cabinet.

At home, I licked stamps.
I sorted wedding invitations
into eleven stacks of ten.

I counted our own days
(one hundred and two).
I comforted impatient
rolls of ribbon,
cupcake liners,
stamped napkins.

Harold Camping Says the World Will End Tomorrow

Sam comes
home from work
at the grocery store.
A woman bought
nine cases of
bottled water,
said she'd be back
with more cash.

I hold his hand
beneath a blanket
that needs washing.
We watch a
mediocre movie
on cable.

Laundry tumbles
in the washing machine.
My fingers fidget
with a loose thread
on the couch.

Camping rented a
billboard down the
street, advertising
Judgment Day.
He listed his hotline.

Midnight nears.
I lie awake, unafraid,
in a bed not quite mine.

Scoliosis Screening, Fifth Grade

We lean in a line
against a row of lockers.
No one speaks.
We cross our arms
over our chests
and slouch.

They've suspended a sheet
between two library shelves.
The nurse carries a clipboard.
The pretty girls snicker at
the one who hasn't started
wearing a bra yet.

I step behind the sheet.
My cheeks burn.
My pink polka-dot blouse
falls to the floor.

"Hands over your head,"
The nurse directs.
"Bend over like you're
diving into a swimming pool."

I curve my spine
for her to study,
curling my toes
inside my sneakers,
wishing only to
point them at the ceiling
and slice through the carpet.

Married Housing

Orange insulation peeks from gaps
in slats of wood with peeling paint.
Married Housing.

On this block, the houses
all look the same: white,
brown shutters,
yellow grass with
burrs that cling
to shoelaces.

The carpet is blue,
commercial grade,
hard as cement,
ripped in the corners.

The kitchen
linoleum is stained,
curling up at the seams.
A huge hole makes space
for the washer and dryer
we can't afford.

The bedroom
is littered with Styrofoam
the landlady can't explain.
"The air conditioner is getting old,
and if it breaks, we can't replace it."

In the backyard, a clothesline
stretches from fence to fence.
A shed leans into the alley.

The previous owners left us
a muddy welcome mat
and two rusty bicycles.
We claim them as ours.
We kiss on the front porch.

Lottery

The line at my register snakes
as an old woman—
face like creased paper,
hair blinding white with
patches of pink scalp—
hands over six greeting cards.

"That'll be $18.19."

She pulls a bursting billfold
from her canvas bag,
searches for a pen,
scrawls an illegible check.

My line filters to another register.
She stuffs a handful of lottery tickets
back in her billfold, her hands
trembling with the effort.

I study the check.
It's decorated with cats.
"Is this phone number still accurate?"

"Unless I win the lottery,
things will be the same
for a long time."

Musings In an Empty House

A faucet drips a steady rhythm in
a rusty porcelain bathtub.
A breeze whistles through the
gaps in poorly sealed windows.
A permanent marker squeals against
cardboard, writing, "Kitchen: Fragile."

I have never paused to hear
the hum of the refrigerator,
the murmur of the hot water heater,
the *squeak squeak squeak* of an agitated fan.

I remember us as newlyweds,
the living room bursting with
wrapping paper and envelopes
as we locked all the doors and,
laughing together,
left my wedding dress
crumpled on the carpet.

I gather nails from the walls,
rub the scars we left.

This house absorbed
the smoke from burnt soup,
didn't laugh at us when we
moved our bed into the dining room
by the only functioning air conditioning unit.

This house offers our memories
in a sealed envelope,
listens for the final click of a lock.

The Last Day Before COVID

March 16, 2020

My sister and I rented a place
for the weekend in Waco:
a novelty dome house
down the road from
the Branch Davidians.

We'd had the trip penciled in for months
and pushed through with our plans.

It was still *there* and not *here*,
but Starbucks was locked
when we tried the door, and
we exchanged wary glances at the gas station
when we saw a man wearing latex gloves.

The unspoken unease rested
on the table between us
during our lunch at the outdoor market,
and I asked her if I should've brought
the surgical masks I'd left in the car.

Around us, skittish eyes shot
to the left and right,
not daring to ask,
not wanting to know

if the forecast was accurate,
if all of this would be in ruins
tomorrow.

On Breaking the Spine of Your Book

After a lecture by Edward Hirsch

You told us of your grandfather's
scribbles inside the
faded covers of old books,
poetry you were too young to read.
Your grandmother's donation
to charity when he died,
oblivious to the labor
tucked in the margins.

Your grandfather might've understood.
A satisfying crack comes
with peeling covers back,
bending like joints
pulled the wrong way
so the pages fall flat,
a dose of poetry
with my morning cereal.

You didn't mention it when you signed it,
nor the scrawls of cursive crowding
your machine-pressed words,
purple Post-It notes
crammed in the binding.

In a messier hand than mine,
you left your name in
bright blue ink,
told me you had
hope for our poetry.

What Happened to Us On South Vernon Avenue

We wanted to buy.
The rent was $5oo cheaper
than any other house we saw,
so we signed the lease
for three years to save for
a down payment.

We should've known when
the property manager asked
us if we were sure, seemed
shocked when we informed him
we planned to apply.

The house was eighty years old
and showed its age in the
sharply sloping floors, in the
peeling brown linoleum, in the
faulty electrical wiring, in the way

the wind invited itself in
through the gaps in the windows.

Here's what happened, and it's ugly:

The landlord took six days to
remove a dead raccoon from
the crawlspace, and when it was
finally gone, it left the stench
of death behind.

A leak in the laundry room

left a puddle immediately,
and the temporary tarp on the roof
stayed there for all three years.

In the second year, we had no
working toilets for eight days,
and the resulting flood brought
a swarm of gnats.

Two neglected trees
collapsed in the yard.
Panes of glass started
popping out of the windows.
The paint peeled off the walls
in huge sheets.
Cockroaches squirmed in
under the doors and
into our beds.

We stayed in that house, knowing
it couldn't protect us from anything

until, finally,
we saved the money,
but it wasn't enough
to buy back
what we lost.

A One-Sided Conversation with Paul the Drifter

He studies Butterfingers and
chewing gum in the grocery line,
his windbreaker ripped at the elbows,
his beard white and stained with
red Kool-Aid around his chapped lips.

His cart holds a blue duffel bag
and a stack of library books.
Cookies, apples, and beer are already
inching forward on the
conveyor belt.

He begins discussing his
brief stint as a steel mill worker,
remembers the clean, crisp air
of his father's farm,
tells me of his plans to work
as a missionary in Ukraine
planting crops for refugees.

"It's important to give back,"
he says. "Like Jim and Patty—
They let me stay for
two months,
no rent."

He pays with crumpled bills
from a wallet crammed
with business cards.
"I collect names," he explains,
squinting at the cashier's nametag.

"Louise is a pretty name."

He buttons his toboggan hat
under his chin and,
mumbling about the
weather patterns of
eastern Europe,
navigates his cart
through the crowd.

House Hunting

Messages exchanged with our real estate agent

Hi, a little bad news…
they chose another offer
but we will keep looking!!!

We can't compete in this market.
Not enough capital,
too hesitant,
too emotionally attached.

Got email. So sorry.
They went with a higher offer.
Let's keep looking.

We fall in love
over and over again
and get rejected every time.

Just checked my email.
This just came to me.
I'm sorry, they chose another.
You can ask to be backup
if they want to do one.

We've got to get out of this apartment.
Our downstairs neighbors despise us
because our kids can't walk, only run,
and our dog won't stop barking.

Hi, just heard… they had 30 offers
and 27 were over list.

I've tweaked the same letter
eight different times.
Please love us.
Please choose us.
I know we're not as attractive
as the others.

They chose another offer.
A few terms were different/stronger.

We're desperate and predatory,
stalking streets online
late into the night,

tempted to drive by and
peek through the windows.

The Giant and the Butterfly

Three memories for Grandaddy

ONE

Sun still rising.
Me: small enough for my feet to
dangle from the wooden chair
in the breakfast nook.

My stomach full of
bran cereal, blueberries, bananas,
I watched you sprawl out
on the pristine cream-colored carpet
to begin your morning stretch.

I followed you to the floor
and settled beside you,
trying to mimic the motions,

but your arms reached wall to wall,
your legs rose to the ceiling.

To me, a giant, and
I felt like a butterfly on your shoulder.

So, I relaxed,
the carpet like a meadow of plush grass,
the sun streaming through the
east-facing windows gentle and warm,
the ceiling fan casting a lazy breeze.

"This makes me sleepy," I said.

You grinned and gave me a look:

No, it said.
This is our time to be awake.

TWO

For my fifteenth birthday,
you gave me my guitar.

It smelled of resin and metallic strings.
The smooth curves of the wood
seemed to hug me back
as I cradled it to my chest.

I knew no chords, but I
plucked the strings—E-A-D-G-B-E—
and the reverberations warmed my ears,
ensnared my heart.

I had found a friend

and that friend has faithfully
followed me through
thirteen bedrooms.

It hangs on my wall right now:
a few scratches,
a chip in the neck,
but still so much
the same
as it was.

THREE

You met him when he was
six weeks old,
a tiny, squirmy thing
with huge, dark eyes.

I carried him into your quiet house
and sat him on your lap.

You studied each other
for a moment,
your hands almost eclipsing him.
He grew still and perhaps wondered,

Who is this
White beard
Plaid shirt
Bright eyes

But you knew him right away—
your first great-grandchild,
just starting his life story.

"Well, look at you."
You poked his soft belly.
"You're just a little guy."

III.

Secrets I Shouldn't Know

Dogeared

On the last page of the
twenty-first chapter,
my thumb traces the crease
in the corner of a page
of a well-loved library book.

I know we're not supposed to, but
it's so easy to just fold it down
and tuck it in, sliding the book
on my nightstand before
switching off the light.

I was once the type of person
who used an embossed leather bookmark,
hand-stitched with a green tassel,
but I lost it on a train in London—
or maybe it's still in the space between
the bunk bed and the wall
in that hostel in Keswick.

I've used Post-It notes and receipts
and old envelopes and
that scraggly bit of paper left over
when you rip out a page
from a spiral-bound notebook,

but my eyes start to blur from exhaustion,
and the crease is already there, so

like a group of weary travelers,
the past readers and I
pause to survey this spot
on the trail and agree:

this seems as good a spot as any.
Let's rest here for the night.

Is It Snowing In Atlanta?

I have the sort of face that
allows me to be skimmed over
in a crowd, until I
blend in with the furniture.

It means I overhear
whispered interludes,
secrets I shouldn't know.

In this airport, I can tell
the man next to me is making
small talk on the phone
with someone who
isn't his wife.

"The flight's already been delayed,
but I don't think they'll cancel it."

It's not my business, but
I stare through the words
on the page in my book.

"I'm looking forward to it, too."

I collect these secrets like currency
from a country I'll never visit.

"Is it snowing in Atlanta?
It's starting to snow here."

Murmurs In the Dark

Your eyes see truths that are not there.
Words form without a page or ink.
You find the strength to calmly care,
you know my thoughts before I think.

Words form without a page or ink,
so draw a line before you cross.
Just struggle for the missing link,
or quickly count it all as loss.

Find me a copper coin to toss.
A hope is hanging in the air.
Or, quickly count it all as loss.
A wishing well is rarely fair.

A hope is hanging in the air.
Like time, it softly passes by.
A wishing well is rarely fair
and has the tendency to lie.

Like time, it softly passes by.
Like love, it often missed the mark
and has the tendency to lie,
but never leaves us in the dark.

Somehow, we're both still standing;
perhaps the lies might've been true.
you're always so understanding,
but I'll never understand you.

The Wedding That Never Was

She called it off with five weeks to go.
"Wedding dress for sale. $500.
Victorian lace.
Never worn."

She spares me the details,
briefly mentions suspicious text messages,
a name she hadn't heard.
"And he never liked my guns.
Or my dog."

Now, she sits on her living room floor
placing ads online.
He took the couches.

"For sale: Glock 19C. Mossberg 12 gauge.
Walther P22. Eight hundred for all three.
Recently went through a big change.
Don't want to sell, but Starbucks pay
just isn't cutting it."

"Don't worry," she says.
"I still want to be
one of your bridesmaids."

I text her late on Thursday:
"I'm here if you need anything."
She replies, "I need time."

Another ad goes up on Facebook:
"Roommate needed. Must like dogs."

Fairies In Catclaw Creek

Morgan—
her name was actually Morgan—
led me through the brush
down to the creek bed
where she had
braided and twisted and curled
the branches of a thicket
to make a tiny cave
shaded by leaves.

I was still young enough that
when her bright eyes shone
and she whispered her secret—

that fairies are real and they'd
accepted the house she'd made them—

I wanted to believe, and asked
if they needed any furniture.

What He'll Find

Her eyes will never be red—
not for him. Not for them.
Not a single tear will trail
down and splash
this dusty carpet.

Five years in Tokyo: sake, sushi,
televisions. His new wife named
International Corporate Finance.

Indiana with a five-year-old,
her mother smoking on the porch
asking about international long-distance rates,
made-up numbers, long silences.

There's pain in the paint
on the empty walls,
darker squares where photographs
watched the scene unfold.
Open windows
litter the linoleum with leaves.
Ants build a
kingdom in the cabinet,
carrying Ritz crackers away
crumb by crumb.

The windows should
be bricked over.
The doorknobs
should rust shut.

Her eyes burn like a letter,
starting at the edges.

FYI

As someone who's spent a
significant amount of time
writing poetry at a
corner table in Starbucks
like a cliché from a bad movie,

I think you should know
the baristas *do* laugh at you
after you leave

when you pull a paint chip you
swiped from Home Depot
out of your purse to show them
the exact shade your tea needs to be
because they always steep it too long.

The Prize

I hear knives in your voice tonight
that carve out hearts and cut them clean.
Your face is pale, your eyes are white—
the sharpest eyes I've ever seen,

that carve out hearts and cut them clean;
my mask will slip, my fear will show.
You are elegant and pristine,
the person we all need to know.

You point a finger, people go
without a thought to their own fight.
As the curious come, crowds grow
stretching endlessly out of sight.

Without a thought to their own fight,
they fought your battle with closed eyes,
but they paraded through their plight
and they have won you as their prize.

They fought your battle with closed eyes,
just answering a higher call,
and they have won you as their prize,
if they won anything at all.

Cities made of steel and chrome
have crumbled to the ground today.
Your wistful words hit close to home,
and, yet, your eyes are far away.

Binge

Wait until you're home alone.
Walk into the kitchen and dig out
that brand new package of Milano cookies
you stashed in the back of the pantry.

Don't take a seat.
Don't make a commitment.
Eat the entire package standing
over the counter by the sink.

Don't overthink it—
doesn't it feel so good
to put yourself first for once?
This is the way you break the rules
since you don't have the guts to
do it in any kind of impactful way.

keep going
check the fridge
eat a slice of cheese
some grapes
those are healthy right
some lunch meat
go back to the pantry
take a spoon of peanut butter
straight from the jar
a handful of Goldfish crackers
no one will miss that
old bag of pretzels you got for
that road trip you didn't take
eat those too

Swallow it all—
the sweetness, the bitterness—

and keep it down.

Coffee Dregs

You, the Intellectual,
scribble a diagram
on a napkin
to illustrate your
Theory of Social Justice.

I nod so you won't suspect
I don't know what you're saying,
but the way you say
"Hierarchal Oppression"
is vaguely attractive.

As you pause to nurse your
Grande Iced Caramel Latte
(skim, no whip),
I ask, "Who's John Rawls?"

You have a meeting.
You're late.
Of course I understand.

This Went On for Eleven Years

She
scribbles shopping lists on
Eiffel Tower stationery:
eggs, saran wrap, instant coffee,
ibuprofen, Cookies & Cream.

He
empties his pockets every evening.
Nickels and dimes added to
crowded pennies, clattering into
an economy-size pickle jar.

She knows
about the pay cut he's hiding.
She buys generic pasta sauce,
puts back the ice cream.

He knows
she sets an alarm for three a.m.
to catch a *Passport to Europe*
re-run on the Travel Channel.

She
tacks a postcard of Prague
on the refrigerator.

He
counts change to
pass the time.

Where Your Beatles Cassette Went in 1993

She loved to snap her
pink corduroy overalls,
slip on her Barbie glitter heels,
wail into the plastic microphone
on her Fisher Price cassette player
to inaudible applause.

My tennis racket,
her guitar.
Teddy bears and
American Girl dolls,
her adoring fans.

It's your fault, you know,
for teaching her all the words to
"Eight Days a Week,"
for playing the harmonica solo from
"Love Me Do"
until she swooned with adoration
for her Daddy.

Four years old,
pigtails swaying,
tugging at a jammed cassette
until I found her
surrounded by
shimmering streamers.

The Healing Under Highway 20

His hands felt baked in the sun,
every fingerprint a paragraph,
each touch a timeline,
rubbing saliva and dirt
into my eyes, a man who had
never seen
saliva and dirt.

Working hands so unlike
those that drive by,
his voice softer than the ones
shouting, "Get a job!"
occasionally stopping at a
red light to ask me how I managed,
without sight,
to write on the soggy scrap of cardboard,
"God bless you for your change."

He was crazy, but so was I—
crawling away,
the melting, sticky asphalt
searing my palms.
I saw
a puddle of stagnant water.

Light, glorious light,
branded into my retinas
the face of God.

IV.

The Natural Way of Things

Grief Is a Loyal Dog

Perhaps the burden of care
has become too much and
you cannot continue to nurture
this limping, trembling creature

who snuggles close at night in your bed,
who begs for food from your plate,
who follows you from room to room
napping softly by your side.

And after all, you did not seek it out
or yearn for it or adopt it—
there on your doorstep one day
it arrived and never left.

So, no one would judge or condemn you if
you took a long drive to the woods
on a rainy Saturday
and shut off your engine there.

If you glanced over to your passenger seat
and stared that dog in its big, brown eyes
and took off its collar, studying for a moment
the deep indentation in its fur at the neck.

If you opened the passenger door and
hauled it out by its scruff into the mud,
and especially if you found yourself
tearing up a little at the short goodbye.

Even if you saw that dog chasing your car
in the rearview mirror, and decided suddenly
it belongs with you—and how could you

ever think otherwise?

It will follow you like a shadow,
nose in your palm, breath on your neck,
your most and sometimes only loyal friend,
until they put you both to sleep together.

The Day My Mother-In-Law Forgets My Name

will probably be a holiday.
The family—loud, excited—
gathering at the table.
The dish by my elbow
out of her reach, she'll ask,
"Please pass the rolls…"

I, the newest addition to her family,
will be the first to go.
My father-in-law will explain
the advanced effects.
I'll nod, sip my water.

When I am the stranger
in her house, I'll find her
misplaced glasses in the dryer.
I'll help her copy knitting patterns
she used to know by heart.
After she goes upstairs,
I'll take the bowls from the pantry
and put them in the cupboard.
I'll track down every spoon and fork
and return them to the drawer.

When her life, like an antique photograph,
starts fading at the edges,
I'll hang our wedding portrait in the hall.

I'll pass the rolls and butter,
make another first impression.

Hospice

Eleven years old—
I didn't know
(could not have known)
what that word meant.

An endless summer
cramped in a house
with fifteen cats,
a mother, two sisters,

a grandmother wasting away,
bony fingers clutching nicotine
until the very end.

1946, Cleburne, Texas,
population 18,932:
"I'll leave here one day,"
she'd tell her friends.
"I'll be an artist."
Long drags from
cigarette after cigarette
littering the asphalt of her
high school parking lot.

"Don't be scared," she said,
"when I lose my hair,
my voice, my mind—
it's the natural way of things."

The preacher explained the word
to us children squirming on the couch.
It sounded like "hospital,"
a place where people go to get better.
I smiled and waved when they
took her away in a hospice van
the day before her birthday.

The Friends You Lose In Your Twenties

Some of them will move so far away,
it's too inconvenient to
stay in touch.

Some of them will be only
friends of friends,
and who has the time?

Some of them you
used to work with,
but you'll all move on.

Some of them won't
remember your married name
and will lose track of you.

Some of them will arrive when you
fall in love, and you'll lose them
in the division of assets.

Some of them will earn
too much money, or not enough,
and you won't be able to keep up.

A few will inexplicably vanish
after something you did or didn't do
(you'll never know which).

At least one of them will
say something Bad
or do something Bad,
and you'll have to let them go
before you're ready,
when you never wanted to.

Thank You

Her son told her,
"I love you."
She nodded, said,
"Thank you."

It's something an
embarrassed teenage girl
says to an
awkward teenage boy
who hands her a box of
assorted gourmet chocolates,
who will later taste the
brittle crunch of toffee,
daintily spit it into a napkin,
use her tongue to pry it
from her polished teeth.

Something you'd hear
a celebrity say on a talk show
to his adoring fans in the audience.

But this was her son.

Maybe there's a secret
her Alzheimer's kept,
a piece of the sentence reading,

"Thank you
for loving me,
even though I can't
quite remember why."

Dashboard Lights

I once let a good friend from high school
drive my old 1996 Honda Accord
down a quiet two-lane highway
outside of city limits.

The lights on the dashboard illuminated
the joy on his face in the dark
as he pressed on the gas and said,
"Let's see how fast we can go."

When we reached 102 miles per hour,
the engine started to groan and I told him,
"Slow down—it can't handle it."
His laughter said, *We could push it,*
but being here and being free
is enough.

He slowed down for me.

I didn't see him after high school,
but I kept track of him online.
When he and his wife finally got
the baby they always wanted
after years of trying,
I wanted to send a gift,
but I didn't have an address.

Here's how the world works:

on a random Tuesday
in Windthorst, Texas,
a young father—only 31—can
die in a tanker truck explosion

with no determinable cause,

and because you were no longer close,

you'll have to watch his family
fall apart on Facebook.

You'll have to squeeze your eyes shut
to remember the shadows from
the dashboard lights,
strain your ears to hear his laughter
over the blaring stereo.

Trapped On a Broken Roller Coaster In Orlando

We round a corner and,
with a jolt, screech to a stop,
a dragon frozen above us.

Some unseen, overbearing adult
paused our movie at the best part.

5 minutes in: nervous laughter.
Taking pictures to post online
with a caption like,
Can you believe this? #thissucks
#feelingthemagic

15 minutes in: the other riders in my row
strike up a conversation as
they notice me straining against
the locked seat constraints.
A kind couple from Minnesota.
An older woman from Australia.

30 minutes in: an unhelpful announcement:
Please be patient. This ride is
experiencing unexpected complications.
My legs, as if in a cement block,
start to go numb.
The man next to me jokes
about getting a refund, asks me
what brought me all the way from Texas
for just one day.

I've always wanted to see it

I've been a fan for so long
I needed to get away

45 minutes in:

I imagine wizards grieve
just the same.
My escape into their world
dissipates with the smoke—
all the lights on,
pale faces staring at
that lifeless dragon
until, finally,
someone comes to get us.

The Folding Hands

For Terry

With delicate care, you folded
two hundred origami pandas
for me to tuck into the programs
at my wedding.

You brought them to me
in a Ziploc bag, all crammed together,
when I didn't ask you to,
but you wouldn't let me say no,
and I didn't want to say no.

You hardly let me say anything—
you barely ever stopped talking,
and I learned to avoid passing by your office
if I had anywhere important to go.
I would get caught in your web and
end up listening to you talk and talk and talk.

I want to bump into you on the street
and stand there on the sidewalk
as you tell me about folding paper cranes
and growing orchids
and how the Green Bay Packers are doing
and what your dogs did
and isn't it awful that they cut the budget
for the student newspaper
and now it's all digital—

but cancer took you, too,
and the little origami panda on the
bulletin board in my office
doesn't say anything, ever.

Yarn

I.

I called it "Old Timer's"
until I was twelve.
I read in my middle-school
science textbook about a
disease that unlearns
everything.

Parking spots,
car keys, hot stoves,
birthdays,
names—

all slowly forgotten,
sand sifting through
clenched fingers.

II.

It doesn't shock me when
my future mother-in-law
comes downstairs after a long
afternoon nap
and pours a bowl
of cereal.

She cannot be convinced
it is 5 p.m.,
dinner in the oven,
sun setting.

Her brain restarted with sleep, and
of course it's 8 a.m.
of course of course of course

and I, vaguely understanding
what is happening,
study my spaghetti.

III.

She loves to knit.
I watch her needles
clink and click
as she watches crime dramas.

She knits scarves for her grandchildren,
their pictures hanging by the TV—
a soft reminder.

Her dogs huddle by her feet.
She calls the name of one
buried in the backyard.

IV.

"The meat is so tender,
you don't even need teeth!"

Easter dinner. She tells the
same joke for the sixth time
that hour.

We try to laugh, but
I see the flicker on her face,
and I know she knows.

V.

Long before her hands
ache with arthritis,
she will drop her knitting needles
and never again pick them up,

her mind
unraveling
like a ball of yarn
tumbling down the stairs.

A Dog Is Just a Dog Until

For Charlotte

she stays up with you until 3 a.m.
locked in your bedroom while
your friends are all having fun
without you in a house across town.
You'd rather be uninvited
than never invited in the first place,
and at fifteen years old, it's the
apocalypse, or should be.
But she rides it all out
with you in your bunker
and wakes up next to you
blinking in the late-morning sun.

Until she turns fifteen, too,
and her hips get too weak to support her legs,
her joints start bowing out from under her,
her stomach stops absorbing nutrients,
she's almost completely blind and deaf,
and it's time.

Until you lie next to her
on a cold tile floor and let her know
the world really is ending this time,
but you're not leaving.

A Candle, A Spoon

We buried you on a November night
under the tallest tree in the backyard
to mark a spark of existence.

I lit a candle for you—
it seemed appropriate, but
the scent was too sweet
and I'll never be able
to smell it again
without feeling sick.
I threw it away.

I used a large metal serving spoon
to scoop away the dirt.
I didn't have a shovel or
anything else useful, and
I don't know why but
we still have that spoon.

I spent over an hour
circling the aisle of
fake flowers at the craft store.
None felt perfect, but I
picked one in the end.

I wanted you to last, but
that flower faded in the sun,
and even that tree dried and fell
one night in a windstorm.

When the Blood Came Back

The first dots of red appear
to reassure you

the hard reset was successful,
operations have resumed, and

although you feel like a
burned out building,
there is still a light on inside,

and not only that, but

the miracle is humming to life,
ready to try again.

Lost, Found, Et Cetera

WHAT WAS LOST

an entire biography
I don't know the ending
or the beginning

WHAT WAS FOUND

another soul to take
an empty space in line

neither equal nor better
nor less than

and a cardinal truth
the opposite of life isn't death
but emptiness

ETC.

the editor in my head
tells me to cut this out
no one wants to read this

no one wants to know
what this feels like

V.

As I Kiss Her Son

Birth Mother

She could be dead

for all I know.
She could be buried in the East,
unintelligible characters
marking her grave.

I imagine, though,
she is still here somewhere—

plump face, sweat,
calloused hands,
dirt caking the
crescents of her fingernails,
hungry mother to hungry children,

his brothers.

In daydreams I picture a new woman,
not the girl who gave him away.
Healthy, glowing,
pulled-back hair,
pinstripe skirt,
cell phone.

She must be aging now,
grey streaking into the
blackest strands of her hair,

the corners of her
brown eyes
crinkling.

She will never know me,
her white American
daughter-in-law.

A dim bar in Seoul.
She nurses a shot glass of soju
as I kiss her son.

Mach 1

When Dad bought his
1970 Mach 1 Mustang,
I would stare at my reflection
in the metallic blue paint,

wait for the deep rumble of the engine
to rattle my ribcage, and
climb in the passenger seat,

the smell of gasoline and exhaust
expanding my lungs until

we took the on ramp
to the highway, and he
let me crank down the window
and hang my head out,

the wind in my hair and eyes and mouth,
the West Texas dust and heat
leaping up from the mirage on the road.

Then he would shift into
a higher gear, and

I swear we left the earth
and soared through the stars.

He'd give me a look like
he never wanted to
take me home.

The Poet On Her Wedding Day

Leather-soled satin flats.
Eight days from twenty-two,
I want to snatch Mercury's sandals,
a lovesick mortal soaring to my groom.

I hear words.
I say words.
Words spring up
in the rims of his eyes,
skip down my spine,
nestle in the grooves
of my fingerprints.
Words jump between
our outstretched hands.

One kiss, and
we are gods,
immortal syllables
ringing from the rafters.
We exit on air.

Dorothy

On Christmas Day my
twenty-four-year-old sister unwraps
a life-size cutout of Glinda the Good Witch.
She adds it to her collection.

Her mind spins towards Oz,
suspended in a cyclone.

Her technicolor thoughts do not translate.
She stammers and speaks of trivialities,
but red shoes slam yellow bricks
toward a wizard to send her home.

She is not well.
Her eyes see past conversations.
She is not here.

She spreads her Christmas presents out
on her rainbow quilt to show Glinda.
I, seven days married, sneak in to say good-bye.
She sets aside her new Hello Kitty sticker book,
watching me drift away in a hot air balloon.

Overkill

Making sense of things is overkill.
With you the world is frozen still
and spinning like a satellite,
us elevated on a hill.

Your precious lips grazing my skin
immediately draw me in.
Inspiration sparks in the night
and pours the ink into my pen.

You are the vision that I sought
the night my soul began to rot,
my battle scars stretched out tight
to show the wars that I have fought.

You are the peace for which I cried
when darkness ate me deep inside.
You are a beacon shining light
when I am drowning in the tide.

I feel your face against my palm,
a beautiful, caressing calm.
My love for you is like a bite
that's turned into an atom bomb.

Some have warned that I'll soon find
truth in the phrase, "Love is blind."
Making sense of things is oversight.
Love can take my eyes with my mind.

Sunset On Mission Beach

He put his head in my lap
and I ran my fingers
through his thick, dark hair,
neither of us speaking or listening.

Together, we sat in the sand
and watched the sun
pass over the Pacific
until the last slivers of light
flickered away.

I checked to see if he'd fallen asleep—
and if he had, I wouldn't have blamed him
after I'd dragged him all over San Diego.

But he was wide awake,
watching the sky,
watching me,

and the breeze turned cool
but the sand stayed warm.

We both agree it's our favorite memory
and often pull it out of our pockets
like a Polaroid to show each other,
to point out the vibrancy
of the unfading ink.

One Vacancy

London runs cattle cars underground, passengers crammed and prodded until it is impossible not to touch a stranger. I see a woman miss her stop because she cannot move. Tourists hug their backpacks, paranoid from friendly advice in their guidebooks. They stumble onto the platform and crowd onto escalators, shoving through until—outside— air, blistering cold, anxious faces in every line of vision. Buses with no seats. Sidewalks without concrete, hidden by shoes crossing the street in stampeding herds before the double-decker buses sweep through, red dragons roaring. Lonely, never alone, losing the thoughts in my head because I have not heard them in months.

I find myself thinking of you

one Sunday afternoon in Hyde Park— dogs, joggers, strollers, lanterns, ducks. The wind bites my neck, so I pull the scarf you once wore out of my coat pocket and leave the path for space, grass, a lone tree with roots shaped like a park bench, plenty of room for both of us.

Post-Partum

I fill out the questionnaire for the doctor
in character as someone who
knows what they're doing and
isn't scared every second

they could send me away
or take you away
they should send me away

I rage against the change
like a sapling in a hurricane
trying to stand up straight
I rage against you

on the phone with a friend
the darkness leaks out of my mouth
in a wisp of black smoke:
it would be better if you had
someone else, someone stronger

I need you so much
as much as you need me
it's too much for someone
to need someone else

my body is broken and swollen
and sewn back together
a monster who spends the night
next to your bed on the floor

you wake me again with your
simplest needs, and it's unfair

to hold it against you
you tiny little thing

I love you
I love you
I love you
I hate you
I love you

Dinner at Rosati's

For our tenth wedding anniversary,
I said we would plan a trip to Europe
or at least a weekend away in Colorado
where we might see some snow for once.

Instead,

exhausted as we are, we manage to
get dressed and mostly presentable
and drive three blocks over
to the nearest Italian bistro.

But, naturally,

we couldn't find a babysitter
(and let's be honest, we didn't try
because it's Saturday night
and it feels too much to ask,

and we're stranded

in the middle of the most difficult year,
and our friends are all child-free
and busy and far away
and won't accept payment regardless).

But it's our tenth anniversary,

so we unload the car, ask for a
table for four with a booster seat
and a high chair and two menus.
The food isn't here yet, but

we're ready to leave

when the baby starts screaming
and the 4-year-old won't come out
from under the table, and
other patrons start shooting looks of

sympathy, disappointment, disgust.

He gets our food packed up
and meets me in the car
where I already have everyone
buckled in.

He kisses my hand from the driver's seat,

his eyes saying, *It's not Europe,*
and it's okay to wish it was.
We hold hands over the center console
the whole drive home.

We used to do that when we were 20.

Helixes

For Taylor

the helixes of our DNA
curl together and
coil tighter as the
floodwaters start to
make us nervous

we move our belongings to
higher shelves and
kick off our shoes

the house fills up
one drop at a time
it will be years
or maybe hours

across the chasm
we grasp for each other
our fingertips brush
until we get a grip
and dig in our heels
ready to leap or pull
the other over

They Said It's Cancer

is something you never want
to hear your mother say
over the phone
while you're standing
in your sister's kitchen.

And since she's your big sister,
she'll let you hold her hand
and then sob on her couch
because you feel some sort of
Ending coming.

And since she's your mom,
she'll text you both later to
see if *you're* okay.

And since you're you,
you'll spend hours Googling
ways you can help,
what you can do,
and refuse to accept the answer:
nothing.

Cookie

MY MOM

has a chocolate chip cookie recipe
that has gained her notoriety in
all her social circles.

The perfect, chewy, melt-in-your-mouth
kind of cookie that leaves people
sneaking handfuls home in napkins.

I

took that recipe with me
when I left for college
and made a batch in my dorm.
Half a dozen friends came with it.

I've baked those cookies for every party,
every work function, for all the
neighbors at Christmas.

MY SON

was a late talker.
We weren't sure if he
would ever talk
and started making other plans.

His first word finally came

one morning in March
when he spotted a full
Tupperware container
in the kitchen.

At 2 years, 9 months, and 7 days old,
he pointed at the shelf
and told me what he wanted.

I Can't Put On Shoes These Days

I bought my first pair of Vans
Slip-On shoes when I was an
insecure teenager who
needed to be the same as
her friends.

        I didn't know I
would buy another pair at
twenty-nine as a new mom.

I've worn through pair after pair
by now, with long walks in our
many neighborhoods, pulling
a dog on a leash, pushing
progressively bigger kids
in progressively bigger
strollers.

        My hands are always
full with blankets and cups, and
someone always needs something.
A baby always sits on my
aching hip.

        Tiny hands tug
on my hair, leaving it in
knots. I twist it into a
claw clip, but he loves that, too.

I can't bend down to tie my

shoes. I can barely find them
half the time.

Like seasons of
war, my resources have been
temporarily rationed.

One day, I'll wear my hair down
and my shoes will have laces.

Intrusive Thoughts During Morning Dropoff

at 7:15, we join the line of
minivans and SUVs

Did he remember his shoes?
Do you remember the time he
got to school without shoes?

he struggles out of his car seat

Is it okay that he's still in a
car seat at six years old?
Why do they make the buckles
so hard to undo?

I hand him his backpack and lunch box

I think I put Oreos in his lunch today

I tell him about the Oreos
he does a little dance

There's a long line behind us

we recite our affirmation words together:
"Kindness. Courage. Self-Control."

I hope I don't get a text from the teacher today

he slides open the door and hops out
and I catch his "I love you" as he sprints
towards the door

and the avalanche in my mind
tumbles down every time:

*What if this is the day
it happens here?*

Third

I want to try for a third
not because we're incomplete
or unfinished

she said you'll just know
when it's your time to know

I know I want you in my life
that the wanting of you
is part of me
whether or not
the knowing you happens

I am a third

and maybe my mother
knew it too
that the empty chair
would always leave her
wondering

Good Sleeper

For Sam

The baby coughs and tugs me from
a blurry dream of soft colors, and
my eyes struggle to find focus
until a car glides past on the street,
its headlights skating across the ceiling
and out of sight.

I wait.

The baby monitor sits on the nightstand,
silent now—just for now—
so I roll over, the old box spring
groaning and complaining

and still, you sleep.

My fingers find your face in the dark,
sliding over the thick hair on your head,
the stubble on your jaw, the ridge of your brow.
My thumb sweeps your lips, the skin there
slightly cracked, your breath warm and slow.

And yes, I slide closer and smell that sweetness—
the breath, the sweat, the everything—
your nose cold, your neck so warm,
your dark eyelashes fluttering,
seeing what I cannot see.

You've always been a good sleeper.
I know I will wake first,
but the rest is mine.

Remembering

Howard Ray Pruitt
October 21, 1926–October 15, 1995
My Grandad

Bernice Estelle Fisher Pruitt
July 25, 1930–July 24, 2001
My Nonnie

Terry L. Minami
1953–November 9, 2013
My Mentor and Friend

Sue Ann Revell
January 29, 1948–November 16, 2014
My Mother-In-Law

Charlotte
June 20, 2003–February 23, 2018
My Beloved Childhood Dog

Sandan Shea Foster
August 4, 1988–September 24, 2019
My Friend

Kieran Shiloh Revell
November 18, 2019
My Unborn Child

H. Taylor Rankin
June 30, 1934–August 11, 2023
My Grandaddy

About Callie Revell

A lmost a lifelong writer, Callie Rankin Revell has been writing poetry and fiction since she was six years old. She grew up adoring Roald Dahl, Shel Silverstein, and any fantasy adventure she could find. In college, she fell in love with modern poetry, particularly T.S. Eliot, and began shifting away from angsty teenage poetry scribbled in her journal towards something more profound and heartfelt.

Callie studied English Literature at Hardin-Simmons University and emphasized her coursework in creative writing and language mechanics. She minored in Communications and Honors Interdisciplinary Studies and won the Campbell-Lacy Creative Writing Award in 2011 and 2012.

When she isn't writing introspective poetry and fantasy, Callie runs her own media management and publishing business, *Callie Revell Media Services*, which she founded in 2013. She edits and designs websites, print publications, marketing materials, podcasts, and more. She feels blessed to be able to make a career out of being creative.

She loves coffee, chocolate, and the color green!

Callie married her best friend, Samuel, in 2011, and they have two children, Greyson and Stellan. They also have a goofy black Labrador retriever named Sadie. They live in Amarillo, Texas.

You can learn more about Callie or send her a message at callierevell.com.